24 Point Circle Designs

by

Judy C. Davis

Published by My Life Press, A Division of Second Wind Publishing, LLC
Kernersville

My Life Press
Second Wind Publishing, LLC
931-B South Main Street, Box 145
Kernersville, NC 27284

Copyright © 2009 by Judy C Davis

All rights reserved, including the right of reproduction in whole or part in any format.

First My Life Press edition published November, 2009.
My Life Press Logo, and all production design are trademarks of My Life Press used under license.

For information regarding bulk purchases of this book, digital purchase and special discounts, please contact the publisher at www.MyLifePress.com

Cover design by Judy C. Davis
Manufactured in the United States of America

ISBN 978-1-935171-71-3

Table of Contents

Introduction	1
Materials, Basic Instructions	3
Blackline Master 1	5
Clean Circle	7
Blackline Master 2	9
Simple Design	11
Blackline Master 3	13
Colored Design Simple 1	15
Colored Design Simple 2	17
Complex Design	19
Down 2, Over 2	21
Blackline Master 4	23
Colored Design Complex 1	25
Colored Design Complex 2	27
Variations	29
Helpful Hints	31
Challenges 1	33
Challenges 2	35
Challenges 3	37
Challenges 4	39
Challenges 5	41
Postscript	43

Judy C Davis

24 Point Circle Designs

Introduction

First of all, thank you for purchasing the 24 Point Circle Design book.

I have always been intrigued by lines and patterns. With a Master's Degree in Mathematics from Appalachian State University and 35 years in the elementary classroom, math has become a part of who I am.

The practical part of this passion came to fruition as an undergraduate at Guilford College. My friends' birthdays came and went, and as a poor college student, I could not provide gifts as I would have liked. I would pass time drawing circles and coloring them. One day, after several people had commented on my designs, I bought a poster board and a Flair pen for less than a dollar. Using a thumbtack to stick through the center, with a string tied to it and a pencil on the other end, I had my compass. I could make very large circles. With these tools, a yardstick, ruler, and protractor, I could make large posters of my designs. They were inexpensive but beautiful. The colored poster board with crossover coloring provided an added depth to the designs. I gave them all away. I doubt that any exist these 40-some years later.

Once I began teaching, I incorporated my circles into my math curriculum. Students loved doing them and did a wonderful job. They were easy and beautiful. My fellow teachers often requested that I come to their class and do a lesson, which I gladly did. The walls and halls soon became filled with colorful, intricate circles.

After many suggestions of, "You should put these in a book!", and 40 years of drawing and coloring, I decided to "share the joy" as they say.

I hope you enjoy these as much as I do.

Judy C. Davis

24 Point Circle

Judy C Davis

24 Point Circle

Materials needed for each student:

1 compass/safety compass

1 ruler or straight edge

1 copy of Blackline Master 1

Fine tip markers or colored pencils

Basic instructions:

* Begin with a 24 point circle with center point Blackline Master 1.

* With a compass, draw concentric circles of 3/4 inch, 1 1/2 inch, and 2 1/4 inch radii inside original circle, using given center point.

* Draw diameters by connecting opposite points on circle. Be sure each one goes through center of circle. For those few students having difficulty, use a copy of Blackline Master 2.

24 Point Circle

Judy C Davis

Blackline Master 1

24 Point Circle

Judy C Davis

24 Point Circle

Judy C Davis

Blackline Master 2

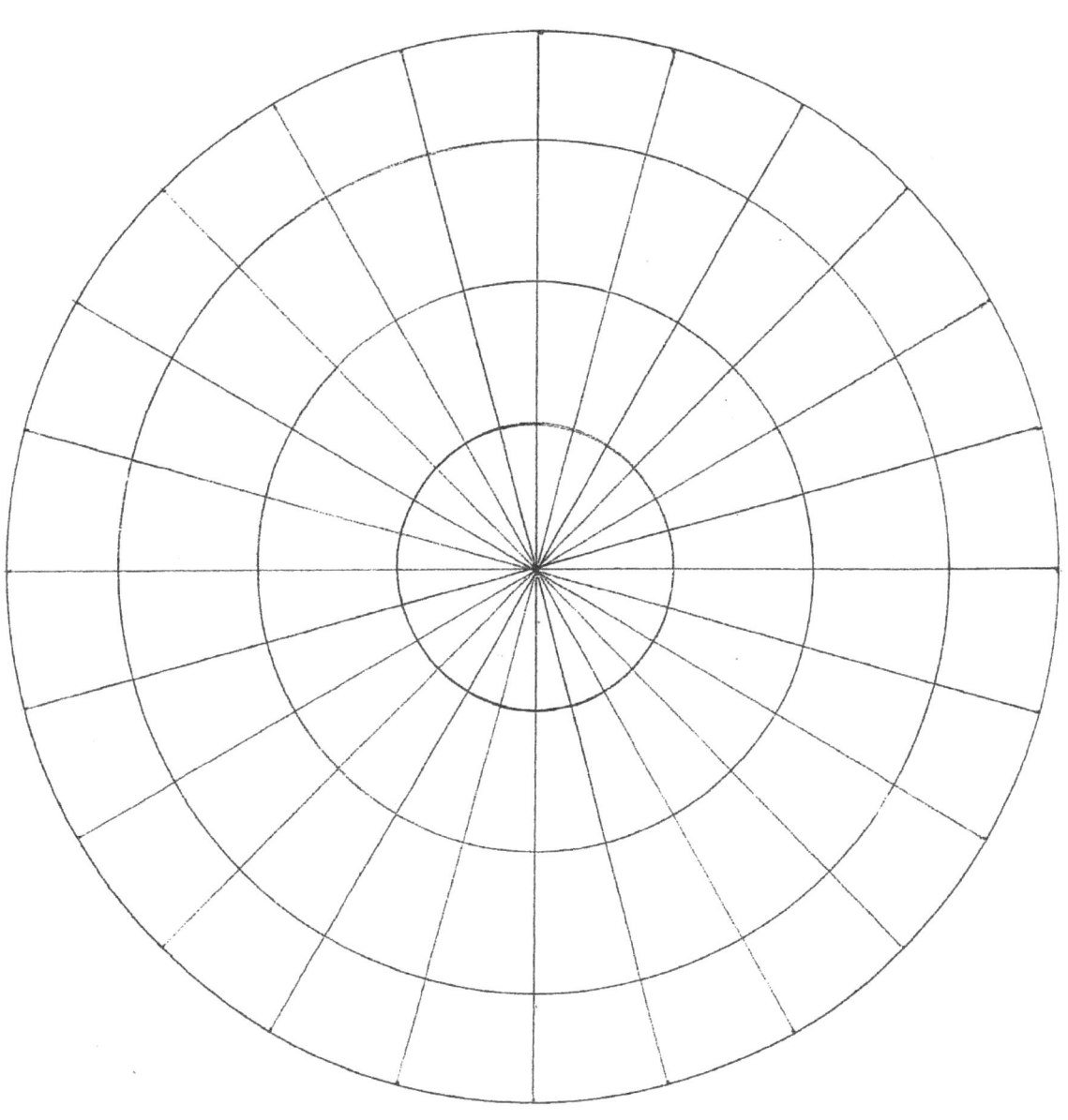

24 Point Circle

Judy C Davis

Simple Design

"X" the Boxes
Beginning with the outside circle of boxes, use a straight edge to connect opposite points of each box, or "x" the boxes.

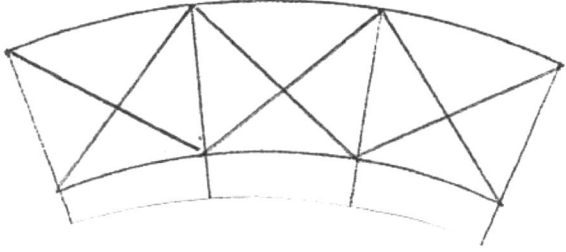

"X" the boxes in the second and third sections.

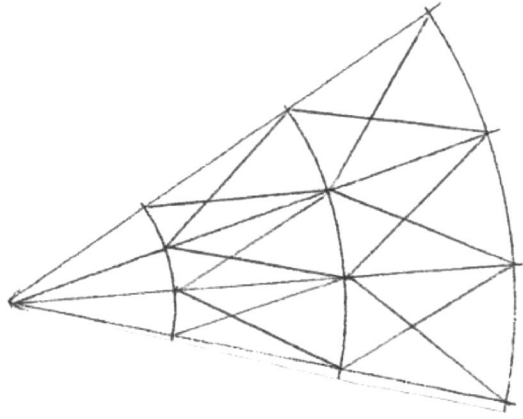

This completes your simple design. Use Blackline Master 3 for those having difficulty.

Color!! 2 to 4 colors work best (factors of 24) for pattern to come out even. Remember white is a color.

24 Point Circle

Judy C Davis

Blackline Master 3

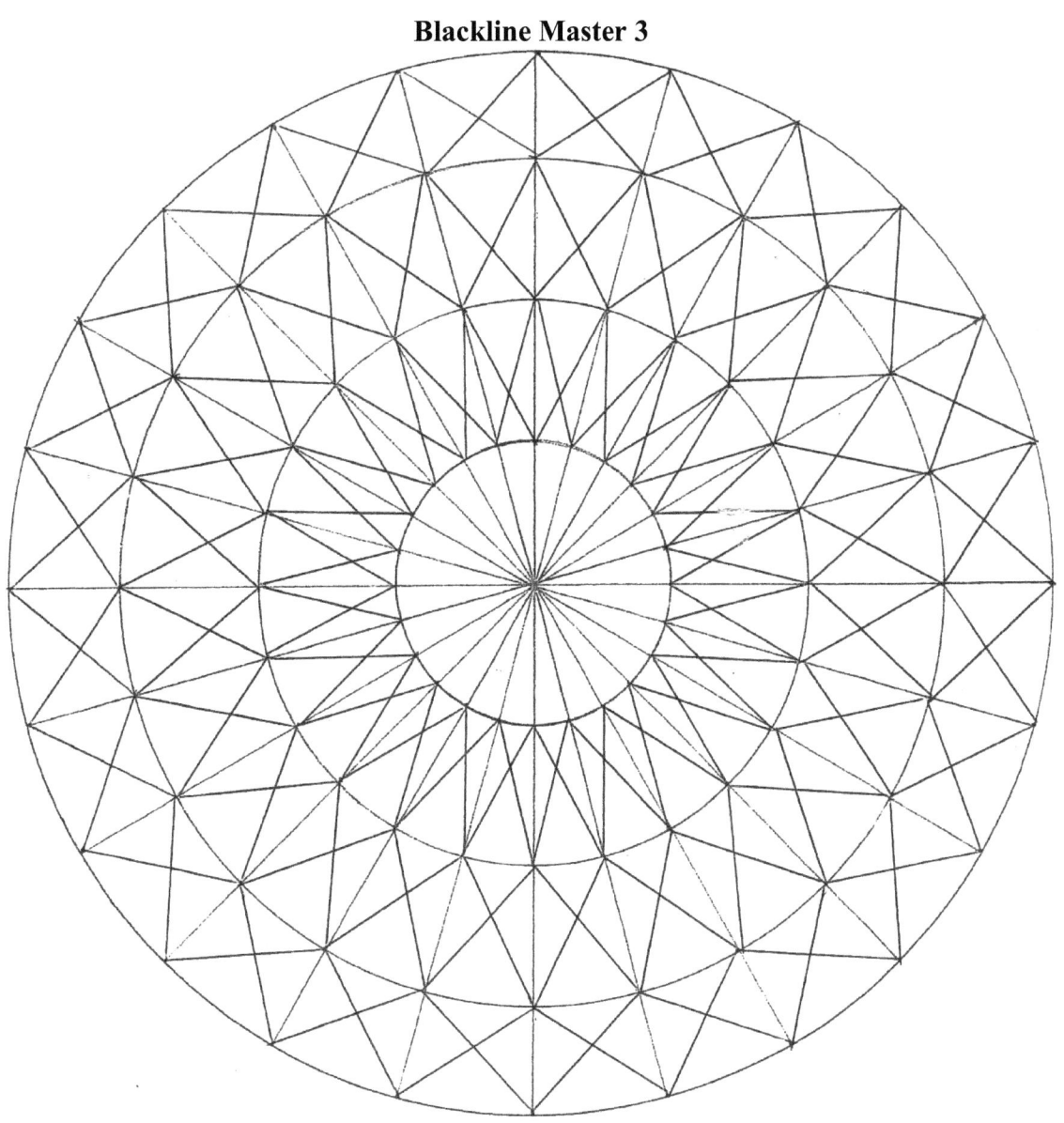

24 Point Circle

Judy C Davis

24 Point Circle

Judy C Davis

24 Point Circle

Judy C Davis

Complex Design

Begin with a 24 point circle with center point Blackline Master 1.

Add circles and diameters as described in **Basic** instructions.

"Crossover" or Complex Design

Design becomes complex when you "cross over" lines to connect your points. This design is the "Down 2, Over 2".

- A. Pick a beginning point on the outside of the largest circle. Go down 2, then over 2 to find your second point. Connect using a ruler. Move to the next point to the right, and repeat to find your connecting point. Continue around the circle.
- B. Starting with the same beginning point, repeat, except go to the left. Connect these pairs of points all around the circle.

You are half done!

- C. Pick a point on the second circle. Go down 2, over 2 to find your second point. Connect. Repeat around the circle. Then go in the opposite direction, to complete the design. Blackline Master 4 for completed design.

See diagram on next page.

24 Point Circle

Judy C Davis

Down 2, Over 2

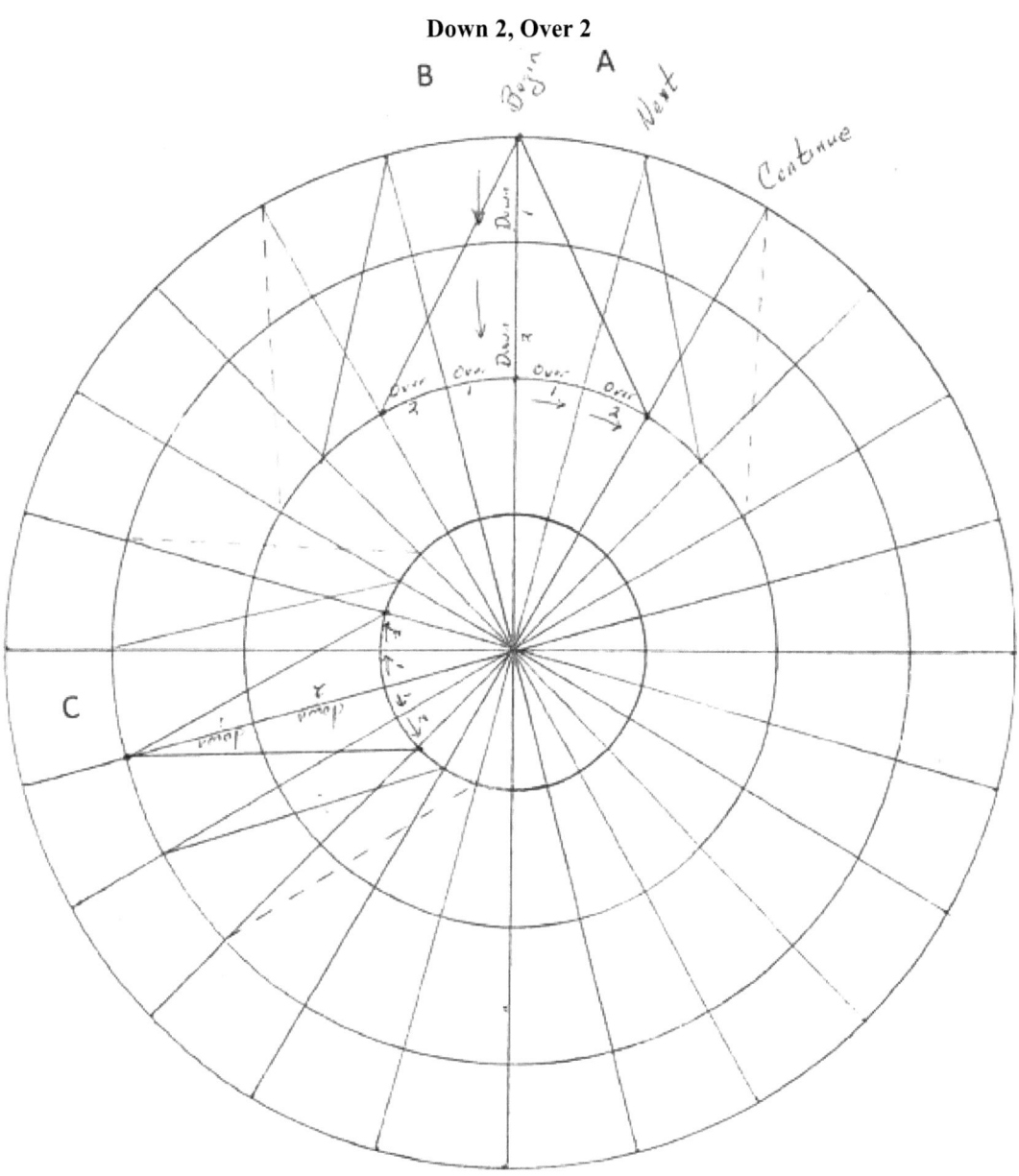

24 Point Circle

Judy C Davis

Blackline Master 4

24 Point Circle

Judy C Davis

24 Point Circle

Judy C Davis

24 Point Circle

Judy C Davis

Variations

Once you get the concept of the 24 point design, the variations are endless.

Complex/Crossover

>Try: Down 1, Over 2
>
>Down 2, Over 3
>
>Go in just one direction
>
>Combine variations

Circles

>Try: Vary the radius
>
>Vary the number of circles

Skipping

>Try: Connect design using every other point (skip one)

Erase

>Try: Before completing and coloring, erase a pattern of lines.

Challenge

>I have included some completed designs. See if you can duplicate them.

24 Point Circle

Judy C Davis

Helpful Hints

Coloring

*If using markers, use fine tips. The sections get very small and precise as you near the center. Also begin with a fairly new marker. You wouldn't want to run out of ink before you finish.

*There are 2 basic coloring patterns. I call them the Pyramid and the Butterfly. Once you begin coloring, the pattern takes care of itself.

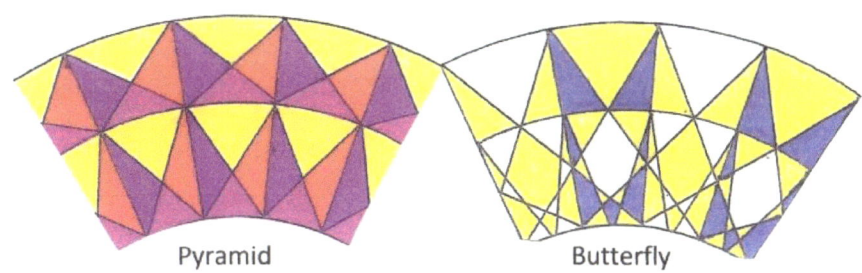

*Save your creation. Once I complete the drawing of my design, I make a few copies before coloring. Sometimes, I change my mind about a color combination, or even worse, I mess up!

24 Point Circle

Judy C Davis

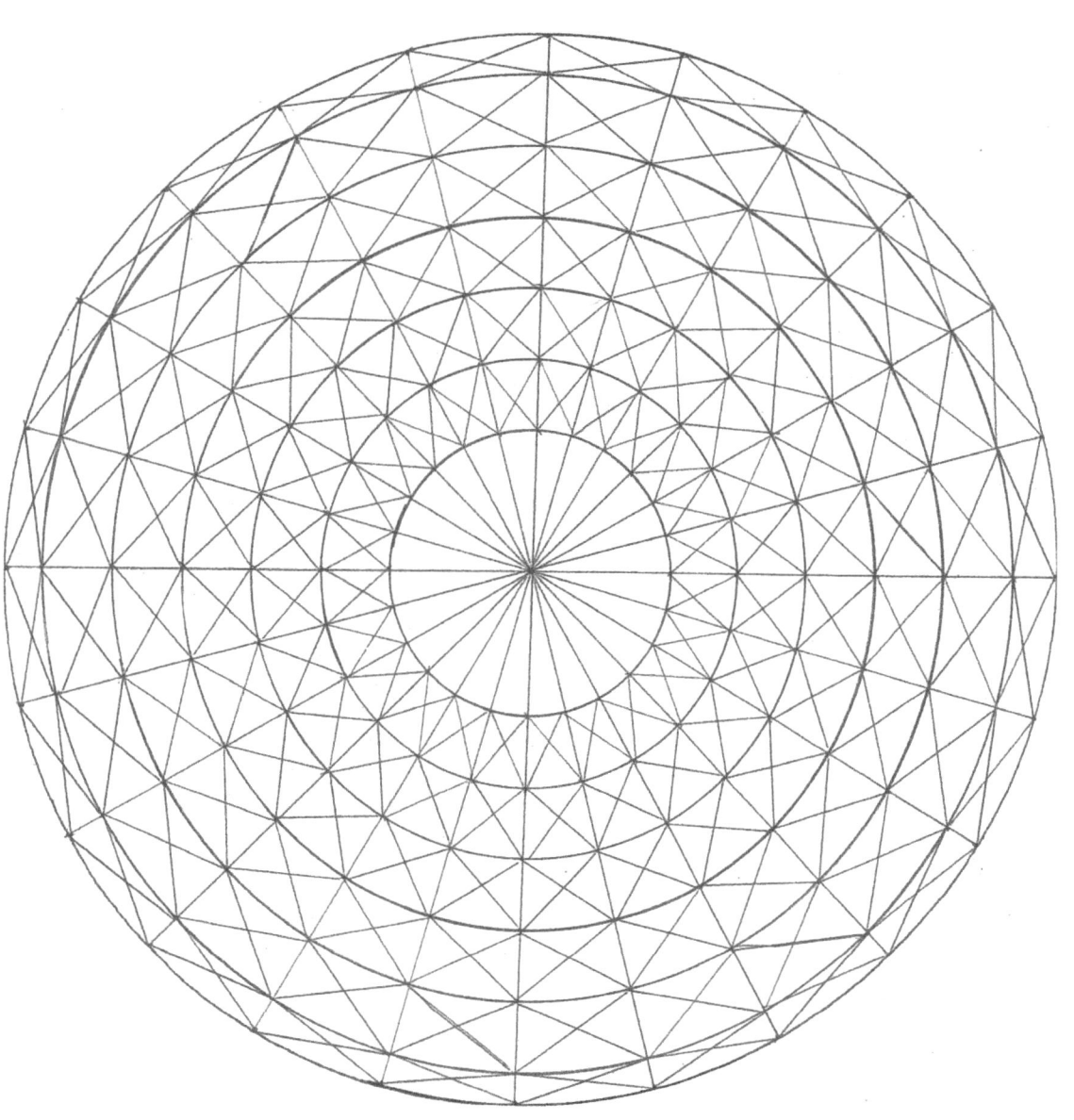

24 Point Circle

Judy C Davis

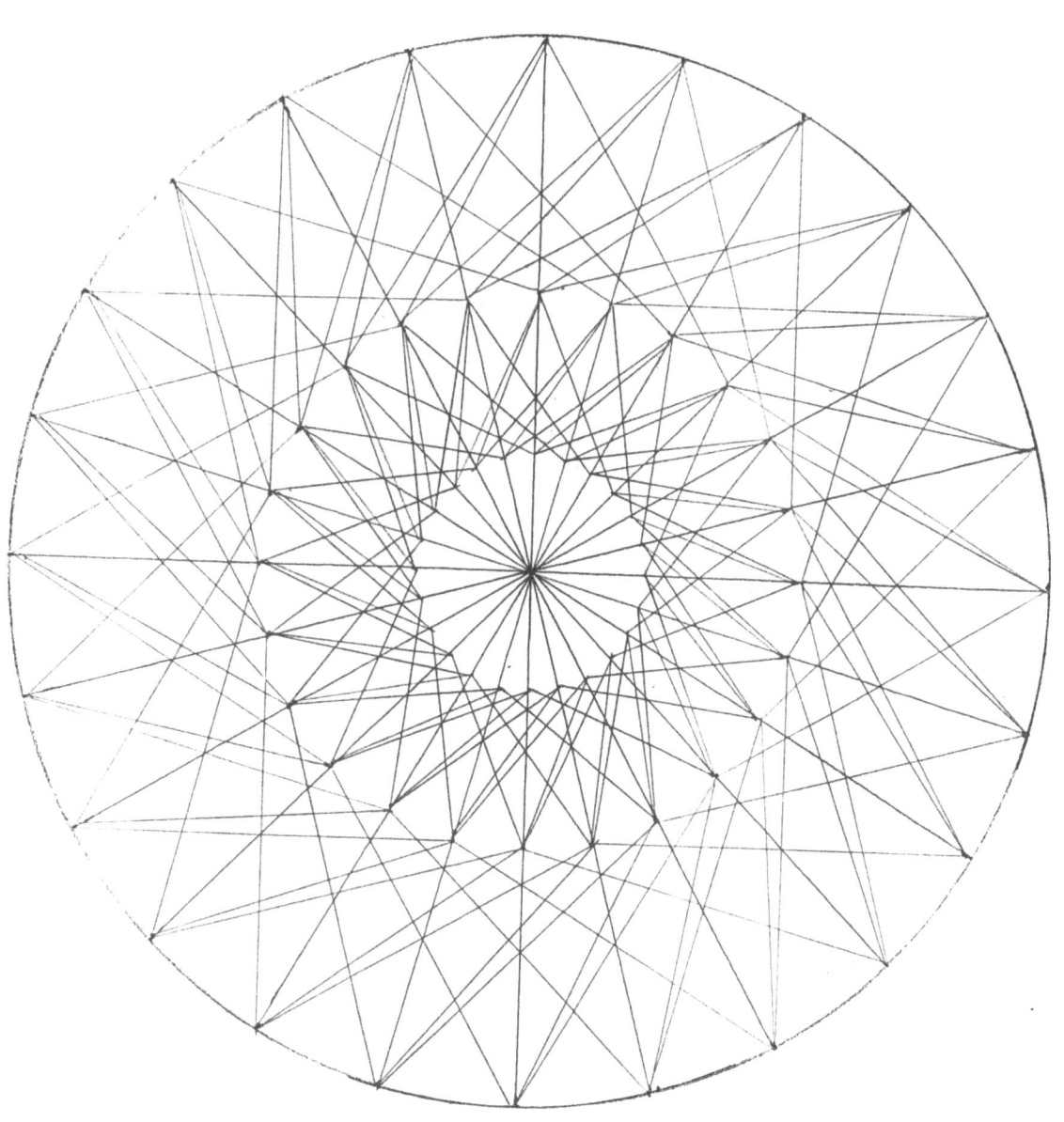

24 Point Circle

Judy C Davis

24 Point Circle

Judy C Davis

24 Point Circle

Judy C Davis

24 Point Circle

Judy C Davis

Postscript, 24 Point Circle Designs

Math/Art introduces and fine-tunes general skills—

Using a ruler/straight edge	Connecting points
Patterns	Coloring
Design	Following Directions

—and promotes

Self-confidence and Pride in work well done.

It also provides opportunities to enhance the math curriculum by repetitive use of geometric terms—

Acute angle	Concentric	Line
Angle	Counterclockwise	Line segment
Arc	Degree	Obtuse angle
Center	Diagonal	Plane
Chord	Diameter	Point
Circle	Divisibility	Radius
Circumference	Factor	Segment
Clockwise	Infinite	Straight angle
Complex	Intersection	Vertex

*Bonus

Fine coloring of designs is very therapeutic for calming nerves and clearing your mind.

24 Point Circle

*Book published by
My Life Press, Second Wind Publishing, LLC.*

For additional copies or to create your own story, living memoir, family treasure, or other printed work, contact Mike at 336-771-2615 or visit us at www.MyLifePress.com

www.ingramcontent.com/pod-product-compliance
Lightning Source LLC
Chambersburg PA
CBHW060821090426
42738CB00002B/64